TRADITION AND MORALITY IN CONSTITUTIONAL LAW

The Francis Boyer Lectures on Public Policy

TRADITION AND MORALITY IN CONSTITUTIONAL LAW

Robert H. Bork

American Enterprise Institute for Public Policy Research

ISBN 0-8447-1370-8

Library of Congress Catalog Card Number 84-62693

Printed in the United States of America

American Enterprise Institute
1150 Seventeenth Street, N.W., Washington, D.C. 20036

THE FRANCIS BOYER LECTURES ON PUBLIC POLICY

The American Enterprise Institute has initiated the Francis Boyer Lectures on Public Policy to examine the relationship between business and government and to develop contexts for their creative interaction. These lectures have been made possible by an endowment from the SmithKline Beckman Corporation in memory of Mr. Boyer, the late chairman of the board of the corporation.

The lecture is given by an eminent thinker who has developed notable insights on one or more aspects of the relationship between the nation's private and public sectors. Focusing clearly on the public interest, the lecture demonstrates how new conceptual insights may illuminate public policy issues and contribute significantly to the dialogue by which the public interest is served.

The man or woman delivering the lecture need not necessarily be a professional scholar, a government official, or a business leader. The lecture would concern itself with the central issues of public policy in contemporary America—pointing always in the direction of constructive solutions rather than merely delineating opposing views.

Lecturers may come from any walk of life—academia, the humanities, public service, science, finance, the mass media of communications, business, and industry. The principal considerations determining the selection are the quality and appositeness of the lecturer's thought, rather than his or her formal qualifications.

The Francis Boyer Lecture is delivered annually in Washington, D.C., before an invited audience. The lecturer is selected by the American Enterprise Institute's distinguished Council of Academic Advisers, and the lectureship carries an award and stipend of $10,000. The American Enterprise Institute publishes the lecture as the Francis Boyer Lectures on Public Policy.

Francis Boyer Award Recipients

1977 *The Honorable Gerald R. Ford*
1978 *The Honorable Arthur F. Burns*
1979 *Paul Johnson*
1980 *William J. Baroody, Sr.*
1981 *The Honorable Henry A. Kissinger*
1982 *Hanna Holborn Gray*
1983 *Sir Alan Walters*
1984 *The Honorable Robert H. Bork*

FOREWORD

Judge Robert Bork of the United States Court of Appeals for the District of Columbia Circuit has long been a lonely but courageous voice within the American legal community, arguing vigorously against the imperialistic tendencies of the American judiciary, and for a return to a traditional, limited view of judicial responsibilities. The American Enterprise Institute's Council of Academic Advisers is pleased to recognize his distinguished contributions to the cause of sound jurisprudence by naming him the eighth recipient of the Francis Boyer Award. The award, named for the late chairman of the SmithKline Beckman Corporation, is given annually to an eminent thinker who has gained notable insights into public policy.

Judge Bork's insights will be needed more than ever in the future, given his description of the contemporary legal situation in this Boyer lecture. He warns us that we are entering a period in which our legal culture and constitutional law may be transformed, with judges assuming an ever larger role in the conduct of American public policy.

There are two reasons for this development, Judge Bork suggests. First, he notes that constitutional law has developed very little theory of its own, and is, therefore, notoriously open to the infiltration of ideologies from the larger society. He cites as an example the ease with which the doctrine of moral relativism moved from the realm of moral theory into constitutional law. It is now, he notes, a widely accepted legal notion that the First Amendment permits individuals to hold whatever private moral beliefs they wish, but absolutely forbids them, as a community, to express those beliefs in law. The Constitution thus simply comes to reflect the notion popular in the intellectual world, that there are no grounds for deciding authoritatively what is right and what is wrong.

The second reason for the possible future transformation of constitutional law turns on the character of the ideologies being absorbed from society by the law, in part as a result of their widespread acceptance within and propagation by the law schools. Such theories, Judge Bork suggests, are dangerously abstract, universalistic, and philosophical. They therefore tend to encourage disrespect for the concrete and decidedly aphilosophical institutions of the American polity. They also encourage us to rely on abstract moral philosophy as the bulwark of constitutional liberty, rather than on the constitutional text and structure, the judicial precedent and history, that have traditionally and adequately protected our rights.

After the devotees of these new legal theories have exhausted themselves in the search for the one, true philosophy of justice, Judge Bork notes, a new danger arises—that of constitutional nihilism. If no universally acceptable idea of justice is available, the new theorists reason, then the judge is free to decide cases however he wishes—to substitute his own arbitrary judgment for the apparently equally arbitrary judgments of the legislature and the people. And that brings us to the final ominous dimension of the new legal theories, according to Judge Bork: their fundamental antipathy to popular government. The theories that prompt judges to substitute personal opinion for law and public opinion are theories that deny the people the major freedom of our form of polity: the freedom of the people to choose and to enshrine in law a public morality.

The way to begin to displace these new and dangerous legal theories, Judge Bork argues, is to develop a counter-theory. That counter-theory would rest on the conviction that the intentions of the Founding Fathers are the sole legitimate premise from which constitutional analysis may proceed. The counter-theory would also insist that the moral content of the law be derived from the morality of the framer or legislator, and not from the morality of the legal theorist or judge. The true morality of the jurist, he concludes, is abstinence from giving his own desires free reign, and a rigorously self-disciplined renunciation of power.

Judge Bork's lecture is a concise summary of views developed over a long and distinguished career in the academy, in government service, and on the bench. He has been the Chancellor Kent professor of law and the Alexander M. Bickel professor of public law at the Yale Law School. He also has served as the Solicitor General of the United States from 1973 to 1977, and as acting Attorney General of the United States from 1973 to 1974. He is the author of *The Antitrust Paradox: A Policy at War with Itself,* and numerous articles on antitrust policy, government-business relations, and constitutional theory. He was appointed by President Reagan to the Court of Appeals for the District of Columbia Circuit in 1982.

Judge Bork has also rendered distinguished service over the years to AEI. He was appointed an adjunct scholar in the early 1960s, then became a resident scholar in 1977. He has also served as the chairman of AEI's Legal Policy Studies Advisory Board and as a member of the institute's Council of Academic Advisors. He now joins a distinguished list of recipients of the Francis Boyer Award, which includes former President Gerald R. Ford, Ambassador Arthur F. Burns, British historian Paul Johnson, the late William J. Baroody, Sr., former Secretary of State Henry Kissinger, University of Chicago President Hanna Holborn Gray, and British economist Sir Alan Arthur Walters.

AEI is pleased to be able to present Judge Bork with the Francis Boyer Award, and we are grateful to the Smith-Kline Beckman Corporation for making possible the award and lecture. Judge Bork describes in this Boyer lecture the "sharply divergent ideas that are struggling for dominance within the legal culture," and thereby reminds us of the importance of the belief that is at the core of AEI's public policy research—the belief that the competition of ideas is fundamental to a free society.

WILLIAM J. BAROODY, JR.
President
American Enterprise Institute

TRADITION AND MORALITY IN CONSTITUTIONAL LAW

When a judge undertakes to speak in public about any subject that might be of more interest than the law of incorporeal hereditaments he embarks upon a perilous enterprise. There is always, as I have learned with some pain, someone who will write a story finding it sensational that a judge should say anything. There is some sort of notion that judges have no general ideas about law or, if they do, that, like pornography, ideas are shameful and ought not to be displayed in public to shock the squeamish. For that reason, I come before you, metaphorically at least, clad in a plain brown wrapper.

One common style of speech on occasions such as this is that which paints a bleak picture, identifies even bleaker trends, and then ends on a note of strong and, from the evidence presented, wholly unwarranted optimism. I hope to avoid both extremes while talking about sharply divergent ideas that are struggling for dominance within the legal culture. While I think it serious and potentially of crisis proportions, I speak less to thrill you with the prospect of doom—which is always good fun—than to suggest to you that law is an arena of ideas that is too often ignored by intellectuals interested in public policy. Though it was not always so, legal thought has become something of an intellectual enclave. Too few people are aware of the trends there and the importance of those trends for public policy.

It is said that, at a dinner given in his honor, the English jurist Baron Parke was asked what gave him the greatest pleasure in the law. He answered that his greatest joy was to write a "strong opinion." Asked what that might be, the baron said, "It is an opinion in which, by reasoning with strictly legal concepts, I arrive at a result no layman could conceivably have anticipated."

That was an age of formalism in the law. We have come a long way since then. The law and its acolytes have since become steadily more ideological and more explicit about that fact. That is not necessarily a bad thing: there are ideologies suitable, indeed indispensable, for judges, just as there are ideologies that are subversive of the very idea of the rule of law. It is the sharp recent growth in the latter that is worrisome for the future.

We are entering, I believe, a period in which our legal culture and constitutional law may be transformed, with even more power accruing to judges than is presently the case. There are two reasons for that. One is that constitutional law has very little theory of its own and hence is almost pathologically lacking in immune defenses against the intellectual fevers of the larger society as well as against the disorders generated by its own internal organs.

The second is that the institutions of the law, in particular the schools, are becoming increasingly converted to an ideology of the Constitution that demands just such an infusion of extraconstitutional moral and political notions. A not untypical example of the first is the entry into the law of the first amendment of the old, and incorrect, view that the only kinds of harm that a community is entitled to suppress are physical and economic injuries. Moral harms are not to be counted because to do so would interfere with the autonomy of the individual. That is an indefensible definition of what people are entitled to regard as harms.

The result of discounting moral harm is the privatization of morality, which requires the law of the community to practice moral relativism. It is thought that individuals are entitled to their moral beliefs but may not gather as a community to express those moral beliefs in law. Once an idea of that sort takes hold in the intellectual world, it is very likely to find lodgment in constitutional theory and then in constitutional law. The walls of the law have proved excessively permeable to intellectual osmosis. Out of prudence, I will give but one example of the many that might be cited.

A state attempted to apply its obscenity statute to a public display of an obscene word. The Supreme Court majority struck down the conviction on the grounds that regulation is a slippery slope and that moral relativism is a constitutional command. The opinion said, "The principle contended for by the State seems inherently boundless. How is one to distinguish this from any other offensive word?" One might as well say that the negligence standard of tort law is inherently boundless, for how is one to distinguish the reckless driver from the safe one. The answer in both cases is, by the common sense of the community. Almost all judgments in the law are ones of degree, and the law does not flinch from such judgments except when, as in the case of morals, it seriously doubts the community's right to define harms. Moral relativism was even more explicit in the majority opinion, however, for the Court observed, apparently thinking the observation decisive: "One man's vulgarity is another's lyric." On that ground, it is difficult to see how law on any subject can be permitted to exist.

But the Court immediately went further, reducing the whole question to one of private preference, saying: "We think it is largely because governmental officials cannot make principled distinctions in this area that the Constitution leaves matters of taste and style so largely to the individual." Thus, the community's moral and aesthetic judgments are reduced to questions of style and those are then said to be privatized by the Constitution. It testifies all the more clearly to the power of ideas floating in the general culture to alter the Constitution that this opinion was written by a justice generally regarded as moderate to conservative in his constitutional views.

George Orwell reminded us long ago about the power of language to corrupt thought and the consequent baleful effects upon politics. The same deterioration is certainly possible in morality. But I am not concerned about the constitutional protection cast about an obscene word. Of more concern is the constitutionalizing of the notion that moral harm is not harm legislators are entitled to consider. As Lord Devlin said, "What makes a society is a community of ideas, not political ideas alone but also ideas about the way its members should behave and govern their lives." A society that ceases to be a community increases the danger that weariness with turmoil and relativism may bring about an order in which many more, and more valuable, freedoms are lost than those we thought we were protecting.

I do not know the origin of the notion that moral harms are not properly legally cognizable harms, but it has certainly been given powerful impetus in our culture by John Stuart Mill's book *On Liberty.* Mill, however, was a man of two minds and, as Gertrude Himmelfarb has demonstrated, Mill himself usually knew better than this. Miss Himmelfarb traces the intellectual themes of *On Liberty* to Mill's wife. It would be ironic, to put it no higher, if we owed major features of modern American constitutional doctrine to Harriet Taylor Mill, who was not, as best I can remember, one of the framers at Philadelphia.

It is unlikely, of course, that a general constitutional doctrine of the impermissibility of legislating moral standards will ever be framed. So the development I have cited, though troubling, is really only an instance of a yet more worrisome phenomenon, and that is the capacity of ideas that originate outside the Constitution to influence judges, usually without their being aware of it, so that those ideas are elevated to constitutional doctrine. We have seen that repeatedly in our history. If one may complain today that the Constitution did not adopt John Stuart Mill's *On Liberty,* it was only a few judicial generations ago, when economic laissez faire somehow got into the Constitution, that Justice Holmes wrote in dissent that the Constitution "does not enact Mr. Herbert Spencer's Social Statics."

Why should this be so? Why should constitutional law constantly be catching colds from the intellectual fevers of the general society?

The fact is that the law has little intellectual or structural resistance to outside influences, influences that should properly remain outside. The striking, and peculiar, fact about a field of study so old and so intensively cultivated by men and women of first-rate intelligence is that the law possesses very little theory about itself. I once heard George Stigler remark with some astonishment: "You lawyers have nothing of your own. You borrow from the social sciences, but you have no discipline, no core, of your own." And, a few scattered insights here and there aside, he was right. This theoretical emptiness at its center makes law, particularly constitutional law, unstable, a ship with a great deal of sail but a very shallow keel, vulnerable to the winds of intellectual or moral fashion, which it then validates as the commands of our most basic compact.

This weakness in the law's intellectual structure may be exploited by new theories of moral relativism and egalitarianism now the dominant mode of constitutional thinking in a number of leading law schools. The attack of these theories upon older assumptions has been described by one Harvard law professor as a "battle of cultures," and so it is. It is fair to think, then, that the outcome of this confused battle may strongly affect the constitutional law of the future and hence the way in which we are governed.

The constitutional ideologies growing in the law schools display three worrisome characteristics. They are increasingly abstract and philosophical; they are sometimes nihilistic; they always lack what law requires, democratic legitimacy. These tendencies are new, much stronger now than they were even ten years ago, and certainly nothing like them appeared in our past.

Up to a few years ago most professors of constitutional law would probably have agreed with Joseph Story's dictum in 1833: "Upon subjects of government, it has always appeared to me, that metaphysical refinements are out of place. A constitution of government is addressed to the common-sense of the people, and never was designed for trials of logical skill or visionary speculation." But listen to how Nathan Glazer today perceives the lawyer's task, no doubt because of the professors he knows: "As a political philosopher or a lawyer, I would try to find basic principles of justice that can be defended and argued against all other principles. As a sociologist, I look at the concrete consequences, for concrete societies."

Glazer's perception of what more and more lawyers are doing is entirely accurate. That reality is disturbing. Academic lawyers are not going to solve the age-old problems of political and moral philosophy any time soon, but the articulated premise of their abstract enterprise is that judges may properly reason to constitutional decisions in that way. But judges have no mandate to govern in the name of contractarian or utilitarian or what-have-you philosophy rather than according to the historical Constitution. Judges of this generation, and much more, of the next generation, are being educated to engage in really heroic adventures in policy making.

This abstract, universalistic style of legal thought has a number of dangers. For one thing, it teaches disrespect for the actual institutions of the American polity. These institutions are designed to achieve compromise, to slow change, to dilute absolutisms. They embody wholesome inconsistencies. They are designed, in short, to do things that abstract generalizations about the just society tend to bring into contempt.

More than this, the attempt to define individual liberties by abstract reasoning, though intended to broaden liberties, is actually likely to make them more vulnerable.

Our constitutional liberties arose out of historical experience and out of political, moral, and religious sentiment. They do not rest upon any general theory. Attempts to frame a theory that removes from democratic control areas of life the framers intended to leave there can only succeed if abstractions are regarded as overriding the constitutional text and structure, judicial precedent, and the history that gives our rights life, rootedness, and meaning. It is no small matter to discredit the foundations upon which our constitutional freedoms have always been sustained and substitute as a bulwark only abstractions of moral philosophy. The difference in approach parallels the difference between the American and the French revolutions, and the outcome for liberty was much less happy under the regime of "the rights of man."

It is perhaps not surprising that abstract, philosophical approaches to law often produce constitutional nihilism. Some of the legal philosophers have begun to see that there is no overarching theory that can satisfy the criteria that are required. It may be, as Hayek suggested, that nihilism naturally results from sudden disillusion when high expectations about the powers of abstract reasoning collapse. The theorists, unable to settle for practical wisdom, must have a single theoretical construct or nothing. In any event, one of the leading scholars has announced, in a widely admired article, that all normative constitutional theories, including the theory that judges must only interpret the law, are necessarily incoherent. The apparently necessary conclusion—that judicial review is, in that case, illegitimate—is never drawn. Instead, it is proposed that judges simply enforce good values, or rather the values that seem to the professor good. The desire for results appears to be stronger than the respect for legitimacy, and, when theory fails, the desire to use judicial power remains.

This brings into the open the fundamental antipathy to democracy to be seen in much of the new legal scholarship. The original Constitution was devoted primarily to the mechanisms of democratic choice. Constitutional scholarship today is dominated by the creation of arguments that will encourage judges to thwart democratic choice. Though the arguments are, as you might suspect, cast in terms of expanding individual freedom, that is not their result. One of the freedoms, the major freedom, of our kind of society is the freedom to choose to have a public morality. As Chesterton put it, "What is the good of telling a community that it has every liberty except the liberty to make laws? The liberty to make laws is what constitutes a free people." The makers of our Constitution thought so too, for they provided wide powers to representative assemblies and ruled only a few subjects off limits by the Constitution.

The new legal view disagrees both with the historical Constitution and with the majority of living Americans about where the balance between individual freedom and social order lies.

Leading legal academics are increasingly absorbed with what they call "legal theory." That would be welcome, if it were real, but what is generally meant is not theory about the sources of law, or its capacities and limits, or the prerequisites for its vitality, but rather the endless exploration of abstract philosophical principles. One would suppose that we can decide nothing unless we first settle the ultimate questions of the basis of political obligation, the merits of contractarianism, rule or act utilitarianism, the nature of the just society, and the like. Not surprisingly, the politics of the professors becomes the command of the Constitution. As Richard John Neuhaus puts it, "the theorists' quest for universality becomes simply the parochialism of a few intellectuals," and he notes "the limitations of theories of justice that cannot sustain a democratic consensus regarding the legitimacy of law."

Sometimes I am reminded of developments in another, perhaps parallel, field. I recall one evening listening to a rather traditional theologian bemoan the intellectual fads that were sweeping his field. Since I had a very unsophisticated view of theology, I remarked with some surprise that his church seemed to have remarkably little doctrine capable of resisting these trends. He was offended and said there had always been tradition. Both of our fields purport to rest upon sacred texts, and it seemed odd that in both the main bulwark against heresy should be only tradition. Law is certainly like that. We never elaborated much of a theory—as distinguished from mere attitudes—about the behavior proper to constitutional judges. As Alexander Bickel observed, all we ever had was a tradition, and in the last thirty years that has been shattered.

Now we need theory, theory that relates the framers' values to today's world. That is not an impossible task by any means, but it is a good deal more complex than slogans such as "strict construction" or "judicial restraint" might lead you to think. It is necessary to establish the proposition that the framers' intentions with respect to freedoms are the sole legitimate premise from which constitutional analysis may proceed. It is true that a willful judge can often clothe his legislation in sophistical argument and the misuse of history. But hypocrisy has its value. General acceptance of correct theory can force the judge to hypocrisy and, to that extent, curb his freedom. The theorists of moral abstraction are devoted precisely to removing the judge's guilt at legislating and so removing the necessity for hypocrisy. Worse still, they would free the intellectually honest judge from constraints he would otherwise recognize and honor.

It is well to be clear about the role moral discourse should play in law. Neuhaus is entirely correct in saying

> whatever else law may be, it is a human enterprise in response to human behavior, and human behavior is stubbornly entangled with beliefs about right and wrong. Law that is recognized as legitimate is therefore related to—even organically related to, if you will—the larger universe of moral discourse that helps shape human behavior. In short, if law is not also a moral enterprise, it is without legitimacy or binding force.

To that excellent statement I would add only that it is crucial to bear in mind what kind of law, and which legal institutions, we are talking about. In a constitutional democracy the moral content of law must be given by the morality of the framer or the legislator, never by the morality of the judge. The sole task of the latter—and it is a task quite large enough for anyone's wisdom, skill, and virtue—is to translate the framer's or the legislator's morality into a rule to govern unforeseen circumstances. That abstinence from giving his own desires free play, that continuing and self-conscious renunciation of power, that is the morality of the jurist.